JOYFUL ORPHAN

Joyful Orphan

POEMS

Mark Irwin

UNIVERSITY OF NEVADA PRESS | *Reno & Las Vegas*

University of Nevada Press | Reno, Nevada 89557 USA
www.unpress.nevada.edu
Copyright © 2023 by Mark Irwin
Manufactured in the United States of America

FIRST PRINTING

Cover illustration: *Swinger* by Ron Kroutel

LIBRARY OF CONGRESS CATALOGING-IN-PUBLICATION DATA
Names: Irwin, Mark, 1952– author.
Title: Joyful orphan : poems / Mark Irwin.
Other titles: Test site poetry series.
Description: Reno ; Las Vegas : University of Nevada Press, [2023] |
Series: Test site poetry series | Summary: "*Joyful Orphan* is a book of witness: species and
   habitat extinction, war, poverty, technology, history, and race. In this collection, Mark
   Irwin attempts to find how these worlds interface and affect one another. There are many
   different ways to become orphaned in the contemporary world, but often it is an attempt to
   understand the meaning of love continuously translated into languages that one does not
   know"—Provided by publisher.
Identifiers: LCCN 2022030348 | ISBN 9781647790943 (paperback) | ISBN 9781647790950
   (ebook)
Subjects: LCSH: Orphans—Poetry.
Classification: LCC PS3559.R95 J69 2023 | DDC 811/.54—dc23/eng/20220804
LC record available at https://lccn.loc.gov/2022030348

In memory of the 5.2 million children rendered orphans by loss of parent

or caregiver during the pandemic as of October 2021.

In memory of those rendered orphan by wars across the planet, especially

those in the Middle East, Africa, and the Ukraine.

And in memory of all the living species and natural habitats lost during

the current and ongoing Anthropocene Era.

For all those rendered orphan through the age or illness of others.

What difference does it make to the dead,
the orphans, and the homeless,
whether the mad destruction is wrought
under the name of totalitarianism
or the holy name of liberty or democracy?
—MOHANDAS GANDHI

Each sluggish turn of the world has such disinherited ones,
to whom neither the past, nor the approaching future belongs.

—RAINER MARIA RILKE,
"The Seventh Elegy" / *Duino Elegies*

Contents

I. Go

Goes	5
Vertigo	6
Balloon	8
The Dead	9
Light	10
Letter	11
Alive	12
Couple	13
Blue, Red	14
Notre-Dame of Paris, 2019	15
Story	16
Livestream	18
Tree, River	19
Hover	20
The Life	21

II. Home

Was into Space	25
Holiday	26
Edges	27
Joyful Orphan	29
Ash	30
The smaller house	31
Arrival	32
How long?	33
Library of Water	34
3D	35
Family	36
Why—	37

We   38
Faces   39
Hungry   40
Radiance   41
Wilderness   42
Bright in June Sun   43

III. WILD

Nike of Samothrace   47
Legend   48
All the tiny arrows   49
Just once   50
Gift   51
Livestream   52
English   53
Plaster of Paris   54
Spring, 2020   55
Nearer   56
Variation on a Phrase by Dickinson   57
Trailer for a Movie not yet Made   58
1937 Indian Head Nickel   60
La liberté libre   61
Thirst   62
Pinprick   63
Three Panels   64
Yet   65
Refrain   66

Notes   67
Acknowledgments   69
About the Author   71

JOYFUL ORPHAN

I. GO

Goes

Goes the jet laying down its shadow, grazing
rapid ground. Goes the clone undoing species. Goes
the email's *whoosh* alone to others. Goes the boy abused to field. Goes
his kite skyward-torn, agape. Goes the clouded mind. Go the soldiers
to Iraq. Go the drones dispatched far before them. Go the blown-out
walls in Raqqa. Go bags of flour among rubble. Go the refugees
broken to Jordan. Goes their God to whom they pray. Goes
ISIL deeper. Goes the orphaned child, othered over
the border. Goes the homeless girl back under the boat's hull
on the LA river. Go the gangs, the Bloods, Crips. Goes the meth,
smack, from Compton to Tallahassee. Goes the OxyC from big Pharm
to door. Go the migrants toward that tear-gassed border. Go
their kids, toddlers too toward their cots in detention centers. Going
with space blankets and without parents. Going strange and long.

Vertigo

The way a good sentence makes light all along
the page, the way a topo map holds sky. I said, The ant looking down

from that piece of apple at its swarming kin. I said, The president looking down
on the broken mob. This table holds part of a life,

even that old wasp's nest appears to be drawn in pencil. Its
vacant cells resemble the abandoned buildings in many cities. I like to touch

its paper shell. The wind likes to budge it around. There are friends
whose names I write now, lighter and lighter in pencil. Just as in the beginning

there's the egg's halving, quartering, eighthing. . .just as in the end
the draining of color, but if you climb high enough on any invisible ladder,

the falling will be a floating down. After her mother
died, she kept blowing up balloons till the small bedroom was filled

and she could no longer move. Thus, cells in the body. Thus, schooling
fish. Thus, boots on the ground and soldiers marching.

Inside every door, thousands of hands opening. Chance
favors those in motion. The female cow followed the red trailer, the one

taking her calf to market, all the way to the property line, and in that *bellowing*, a new
frontier of language, and I sensed the way words can become

a net of being: Morning—the brook trout's leap carrying all the luck of light,
its brief tattoo on the lake. And the wasp's nest

blew off the table. And parts of one city collapsed into the ocean.
And the balloons drifted all over the house. And the girl opened closet

after closet until she found the one with grass, cows, and a lake
the trees kept tamping down.

Balloon

That we are instead of darkness,

that the light is steady, hard, even in far Decembers,

that the word *April* drills outward like rain in its own incandescence,

and the downy woodpecker's drumming, the shrill *che che che* opens new spaces
around the shagged cedar,

and that ruddy cow—leaning to sup from the Arkansas River—has
a thirst equaling ours for memory,

or that *laughter, laughter* echoing around these canyon walls,
or the *laughter* leaking air from a red balloon

as fast as the weight of one body toward a teaspoon of ashes
that will never compensate for her excess,

and now evening light streaming across this wall tells me I am nothing,

and now moonlight filling in where the sunlight was,

and now a father's hat still opening like a parachute over my head.

The Dead

Yes, it's like this. You are walking in a field, and the field's
gathered by a few trees that become a sun-splintered
woods, and then after your father staggers in the yard, a mother
goes, perhaps nursed long by a sister at home, the woods
become forest, and when that lover—first kissed beneath
a fire escape's trellised pattern on W. 45th St.—dies in Paris,
those spruce grow taller as you see again the five oranges
spilled from her bag, rolling across the green carpet
where you both crawled, mute animals, in that room grown
wider by grasp, more desperate now in memory, in this
steep shadow, where those oranges, minus the one
shared, carillon briefly, eating darkness, making a shell
of burnished light where you can kneel and begin to listen,
hungry again for those raw, pressed sounds to make the dark shine.

Light

—so much light the gunman can't find his target,
and an animal comes out of the woods and wipes its paw
over that man's face. —He, the one who wakes into another
life. And though I say *he*, I mean *they*, all of them, *us*,

who somehow pull the trigger, tall as someone
we almost touched in the mall that day
by the fountain, drowning out everyone's voice
into one. —I remember walking once at noon through a crowded

park where a young homeless woman was sleeping
on the grass and she said, "Go on, come closer and see
what happens," and I keep thinking about that space, her
space—anyone's violated space become

a room collapsing, and I'm thinking how
the light never hurries to end, unlike words
that somehow need to keep opening like this forest
so that the first animal might come.

Letter

Times when we touch hope like the hem of a cloud
just as when we touch a body or door, or think
of the dead come back, romancing
us through the warp of memory, lighting a way
by luring, and that's why sometimes
I'll walk far, saying *is* and *was* over and over until their sibilance
becomes the fuse of all I know. Yes,
you might ask, "Where was
I when the world laid out its dimensions?" The dead chimp at the zoo. How
the other chimps gathered around, and one laid a creased hand
on its forehead as if taking the temperature
of the land, a grief arriving from millions of years
like a letter we keep trying to open, or Mary's letter
I found in the mail—returning from a long trip—after she
had died, and how by not opening it for weeks
she remained alive, then her words arriving through the white folds
like blood from a cut, vivid consonants, vowels
combining as if from cells dividing—life hovering and then
nothing but the wound—words—and I remembered how the Javanese do not
utter the word *macan* (tiger) after dusk for fear
of waking its presence.

Alive

She sang—I mean she tried—for she, tired, could
no longer hold a tune, as the brain synapses slowed
with age, a minor stroke, Parkinson's, and broken
collar bone canting her a bit starboard side, she
sang a song—broken like her body—holding some
notes a long time, millions of years in fact, the way
granite holds intruded gneiss threading its cursive
path toward sunlight, "I feel so alive," she kept saying
between sloppy chords, "I've never felt so alive," as
she sang, "What a wonderful world," though nothing
seemed that, and yet it was, her veins purpling
around senile lentigo spots on hands jumbling by
her face, as if the tune were a net, a beautiful
net she was just now lifting off for me to hold, I mean
to practice holding for other songs still arriving.

Couple

After bad love, she vanished into the forest with her son,
her son who was more like a woman in that the river stones
became soft in his hands, and together they made a house
with them, and a roof of sloped tree limbs and moss, and they
brought no smartphones, laptops, or books, but a telescope,
pencils and papers for drawing, writing, and they told stories
to one another at night, stories about migrations, her favorite
of his, a herd of horses turning more and more green as they
ran through fields; his favorite of hers, the stick people
that built stick houses in autumn, and so disappeared into those
thatched houses while her son continued to draw the night sky
by penciling everything in until the paper was black except
for the pricking lights of those constellations to which he added
the moon, Saturn, and Venus, all while a great diaspora occurred—
people scattering from cities, many moving toward the mountains
where million-new-jeweled lights appeared among scattered fires,
smokestacks, as the animals fled in opposite directions and the mother
and son watched until the mountains became cities, some warring
against others, and as the boy wrote about this, he resembled his mother
more, their long hair sweeping over the green until they wept from one body.

Blue, Red

Winter, and in the time I'd been traveling home
the snow had grown deep. I shoveled around
their house, and when I entered, Father drew a red
line across the living room floor, and mother drew
a blue line across the kitchen's. *Come*, each one said,
and I went into the kitchen first because I was hungry,
and there, mother taught me how to read, sing, touch
again, and she fed me till I was fat, happy, till the blue line
disappeared, and father called me now again. He had
grown a beard and hunched by a chair where mother sat—
her blue eyes, gray. *Come*, Father said, and the red line
had grown wide like a bed, and now they both kneeled,
their eyes asking of some far-away where a dog barked,
the bark slowly filling the darkness, and then mother lifted up
the hem of her skirt and pushed a suitcase toward me,
and I took off my clothes, folding them into the suitcase kept
now in the closet that I keep opening and closing where the red line was.

Notre-Dame of Paris, 2019

Its spire in flame, an orange hat we all wore, watching the pompiers'
water cannons stream against flaring

hotspots that produced a thick smoke resembling lava

rising from the geological past where 3,000 shovels & pickaxes once dug,
erecting the Gallo-Roman temple to Juniper, and later

the partial foundation, a Christian basilica, followed by the St. Étienne Cathedral

on the now Île de la Cité, where Louis VII began it in 1163, a 200-year project
that would survive the French Revolution, two world wars
and now this roving

fire—leaping among rotting joists and new scaffolds—crowning a center

where the spire's tongue might lift off like a NASA rocket. —An Event
Horizon. Easter, six days away and one year before

2020's Holy Week & congregations that will be culled by COVID-19, Paris
near-emptied, as Archbishop Aupetit delivers the Good Friday Mass,

accompanied by six others, all white-helmeted upon entry, with 3 performers in
    hooded
virus-suits for the presentation of the Crown of Thorns, spared by fire, as a violinist
plays Bach, and 15 million watch within their own quelled sunlight.

Story

She wanted to write a story but wanted it to be new. Once in Alaska
she watched for an hour the vast Columbia Glacier
melting into Prince William Sound. In 200 years
it had retreated 13 miles during how many
wars? She pictured a burning fuse next to a glacier
melting, and how it becomes harder and harder to find the future
of that story. The great arena of freedom
like that of a bee moving within the bell of a day lily, its feet
and mouth turning around anthers, its
pollen-dusted body, light-intoxicated. —To stay

or leave? In church once, the choir singing Mozart's *Exultate*
Jubilate, she heard a jet coming over low that drowned
out their voices along with the organ. Mouths
moved with no sound. —Song, turbine-undone
till the soprano took it back, slow,

the way a planned park will take back a landfill. Fresh Kills, she saw it first
in the mid-80s on a trip to the Statue of Liberty, the trash dump
becoming the largest manmade structure in the world, built
like a layer cake—fresh trash covered with burnt trash
covered with fresh, 80 feet higher than the Statue of Liberty,

and she thought of the Columbia Glacier again, but as something
alive, a breathing, feral thing. The landfill, phasing
out around the year 2000, reopened for 9/11. Forensic teams digging
through debris for body parts. A cell phone ringing among
trash, weeds. —Digital, vegetal. What iPad or ledger vast enough
to record this? This new brevity of screens, a lingering
once, archive of all, for any event to be played

again, but one artist, Marguerite Kahrl, assembled from landfill parts
a remote-control vehicle that runs on garbage's methane gas,
a vehicle taking back control, like the soprano,
notching pitch up a bit, the vehicle that will soon
roll through the verdant park, once dump—a dilated threshold

like the one Vaughan Williams creates in his *Pastoral Symphony*, the fourth
movement that begins and ends with a voiced but wordless
soprano, marked "distant" on the score, and where—between the two passages
of her wordless lament—ghost soldiers rise,
many of them the composer's friends, through
the French countryside where he used to drive the ambulance
"at Écoivres and went up a steep slope and there
. . . a Corot-like landscape in the sunset." —Those muffled drums
like boots on the ground just before the soprano
starts singing the high hymn, far, like a fuse burning on a glacier.

Livestream

In sleep, snow fell and for each person that died
   the house lifted. The years, their incomprehensible weight
of feathers, and when a horse stared in the window, I rode
   off with my sister, two girls galloping
toward the city—all the freedom one could want—till the digital
   blinked on every screen, the horse now a splashy
lithograph on the wall, soon to be auctioned on eBay while
   among honking horns I've grown old, homeless and sit
   in a park where once I gave birth
to a knight who—bleeding—still wanders from city to city.

Tree, River

"River of life, tree of life, which would you choose?" What? I asked,
hoping she might have said, "the house, or summer cabin, which would you like?"

So, I drew a tree and below it a river, then erased them both, and in that erasing
I heard wind. —Between birds in flight, the void of something I want. *Schhh,*

she said to me once when hiding together in a closet to surprise her sister's
husband. Just the birthday candles lit the dark.   To avoid speech
I thought, the trees—*Schhh, Schhh.* She dreamed,

delirious, toward the end, and talked about the farm, her 4-H pig, Willy,
a Cochin hen named Granny, the patch of 7 sunflowers planted dead-center
in Daddy's alfalfa field with the secret alleyway toward that sun-hive where she kept

her dolls, and the way she recounted it all, there being no difference
between memory and death. Yes, the river—hers—everyone's.

How many million years in a river? And we—just a creek—flowing into it
when like apes we walked on our fists. *Tree, river.* Water, sap, blood.
Even with our bodies we *present* its past, its marrow of shadow and fish

sourced from mountain snow that will make some limbed, branched thing
grow tall in a valley, and sometimes you'll hear

a man and woman talking, staring at the generative leaves
and wanting a child. Life—*you*—more than that to me.
You, river.

Hover

If you hold the ladder's wooden rungs tightly as you climb,

you can feel how it evolved through 10,000 years from staircase to elevator

& if alone you close the elevator door and scream, no one will hear you

as you rise to the 79th floor balcony and—looking out over

the city's millions of staircases and ladders where people climb up and down—

you may feel a sense of power but loss of freedom until night arrives

and people begin to lie down and their sleep flattens all things out

into a far, over which only the infant trees keep watch.

The Life

I have no house and live in the forest.

I know your language but no longer speak it,
though I often hum, mewl, or mimic the trill of birds.

The cardinal's I like best—*twuuu, twuuu, twuuu*—three long silver notes,
a temporary bridge, spanning the air.

Like you, perhaps, I buried a mother and father, and now walk their vast terrace.

I eat mushrooms, fish, and leave no footprints.

I have no money or belongings but make drawings in the sand.

I am my own house through whose windows and open doors you have glimpsed
a deer or fox's gaze

and my sex is one green equal to the age of light.

II. HOME

Was into Space

There was the time in August when guests from the wedding down the street knocked by mistake at the door where the funeral reception was being held. We tried to ease their shame but cars follow bunches of parked cars and the small spaces between each like that grief among us.—And there was the long-ago space beneath a bed where sometimes the boy hid between a box of clothes and a rolled-up rug, a safe space where toy Indians roamed among dust clouds, and there was the closing space he'd glimpsed between two joined bodies as he closed a door, and much later in the story he continued closing the space between another body and his, a riding of sorts to nowhere, the same nowhere he was left with after she leapt toward a teaspoon of ashes he kept in a small plastic sack inside a silk one next to his socks because his legs had no feet and stayed put for a while till he decided to swim back and forth in another space, eighty laps, two miles, to distract him till one snowy night he made a fire out back and could see the space between lit flakes melting as he made the fire bigger, adding more cedar, wanting to toss her ashes back into the fire from which she'd arrived, to remake her space, letting it become mobile—see, they were *there* and *here*, both once a *now*—remembrance joining discovery, reaching across the years.

Holiday

When the grown kids would come over
with their kids, and after their kids left, and the plates were cleared
and the years spindled on, and only the mother, now
a great grandmother and I remained, an enormous cake the size
of the dining room table appeared with icing more white
than our hair, and we entered the cake, which kept growing, with our
hands, and found necklaces there, rings we put on as we fed
one another—reading from the cards we found too—the cake now
the size of the entire room, its frosting staining our lipsticked mouths
as it continued to grow and we crawled inside its vaulted rooms, where in one
we made a fire and drew birds, deer on its walls, and the fire,
yellow at first—but not hot—grew larger, becoming
green, and we entered its immense field where we walked
until we came upon a tree, towering above, swaying all red
in the wind, and we did not stare at it for we felt
both inside and out, but had no idea where.

Edges

After the body's put in the ground, the bells pealing, baffling
air, buffing it, almost bluffing as if they
could say more, and then

the seconds turning to iron as the faraway
becomes close in memory, and what seems needed now,
a giant tortoise to crawl over the broken ground and flowers,

confusing the fabulous present, which some scientists
believe is still continuing since the universe
began, and if it is, then no

one really dies, right? Just the contours and boundaries of things
give way—a body. Or as when rock and stone
in great heat become elastic, the way

those bells sounding now become elastic in air and suddenly I'm
looking for the edges of myself, thinking
about place, that plastic

bag blowing, lofting, unable
to decide where to
put its

mouth, what patch of grass, or concrete
the moment might fit like that beetle
in a robin's beak. Yes,

like that, or her face I almost knew by rote as that tortoise
plows between calyx, grass. —What is a foot
of time, an inch? In

one dream, three of us sitting in the grass are making hats
from newspaper when a great wind
blows them off, everything

round and round the lawn, paper clinging to trees,
and you screaming—voiceless—no
sound.

Joyful Orphan

While many are starving,
shopping bonanzas bourgeon each minute
online. —Detailed photos of everything for sale or not—a two-carat emerald-cut
Moissanite set in white gold, the red valleys and craters
on Mars, a macrophage's
splayed slime engulfing bacteria, or perhaps your own
mutated cells. Do you really want
to see this? Or your exact meal before
traveling to eat it next week? *Before,* once that word meant something
different: Cook staring off the Oregon coast
into the fog. —Or beyond *Voyager 1* entering intergalactic space. There is no
more difficult space than the ones we've lost, those green spaces,
the oceans, the polar ones too we paste
on our screensavers, our roving minds roving after what's
gone, then filling them. Now I want a tiny house that fits on my body
like a glove. To be lost in any
forest again where the only choice is to walk toward
a river's undocumented
sounds, its eddies and currents, its luck
in the rain opening.

Ash

They stood beneath that tree and talked, the same tree
they stood beneath when his father died and when his sister woke
one morning and could not walk. The tree, a Patmore ash, he'd
planted with his neighbor, Jack, thirty years ago, backing his Jeep through
the back gate, the two of them lugging it toward the fresh-dug hole, the hose
making fresh mud, pooling where they tilted the bole, centering the root-ball.
From a woods-distance one might think they were on their knees, sipping
at a spring, or lifting the mast of a sodden boat toward where? And there's the limb
halfway up, sawed off after Jack's son, Tom, fell 10 years ago and broke
his arm. They both knelt beside him as they knelt when planting the tree.
One April midnight, he'd watched meteors shower briefly through
its ghost-branches, and once in 2011, he saw Scorpio rising in the south
between its barren limbs, Antares' red eye lifting its hook
through autumn's remains, and it was under this same tree that he'd called
Mary, inviting her to dinner. In route that Friday she was hit on the freeway, her
car totaled. She was OK, but three years later died of a stroke. She'd
wanted to have the dinner at her place. Why did he insist? —The way
the frost does now on the butter-tinted leaves that form a vast
tent, where he'd once hung lights when his daughter, Heather, was married.
—Everyone clapping and dancing. And there's the woodpile, limbs sawed up,
stacked after the ice storm five years ago—the wood he adds to the backyard fire now,
its silk doors shifting as he shifts in and out of the past when before he'd planted
the ash, a blue spruce—half beetle-killed—stood over fifty feet high, and how
he'd helped Duane, a hired hand, take it down over three June days,
sap all over their clothes under the collapsing resinous green vault, ghosted
still, as he adds some of its split kindling to what's tongued—twinned
in tasking embers, mating flames, doorways fruiting farther light.

The smaller house

While building the larger house he lived a very simple life
in the smaller house he'd built before, the house without
water or power, the 12 × 20 ft. house with three windows,
a single bed, chair, the house whose thousand books lined
the walls, including some he'd written in the house, written
by window light, or the Coleman lantern charged each day
at the hot springs pool, where he swam every morning, and now
living in the larger house with every convenience, he missed living in
the smaller house with none, where sometimes he'd lean against
a dusk-window just to finish a line, or where once in the dark he wrote
in pencil a dream on the wall, then went back to sleep, finding
later those words like a string in the forest in the new light.

Arrival

Visiting once, I arrived late and Mother asked, Are you
hungry? Yes, very hungry, I said, and in the kitchen's dusk
she opened the refrigerator door but there was nothing inside,
just two heels of stale French bread, and then she asked, Would
you like a sandwich? Yes, I said, a sandwich would be fine but—
Don't worry, she said. You always were such a worrier. And
then her hands caught fire—small blue flames—and she appeared
to be cooking something between them. *There*, she said, a *chicken
sandwich*. I ate ravenously, though taking small bite
after bite, making the meal last, as we stared at one another
in the dark, lit only by the open fridge, its stubborn moon.
You must be exhausted after that long drive, she said. Yes,
I mumbled, staring at her pink hands, perfect except for crumbs,
and then we headed toward our rooms, mine down the hallway, hers
that starship—outside the patio door—hovering in a copse of trees.

How long?

Between yesterday and tomorrow, I keep trying to get closer,
between lights out and reveille, or that moment in dream
when the apple in your hand stretches for miles with the snow's

tart flesh. —Or when skin awakens, loin to loin, and a jay's
signet-cry hangs in the air while ants, insistent, rebuild a tumbled
mound. —Kindling, as it bursts to flame, or the alphabet spilling

from a child's mouth. How things keep enlarging the breezy present.
How long before the number of dead replace the living on Facebook?
—Bees swarming around a new-released queen as the glee club holds

a sloppy hallelujah. Rembrandt drawing the dying Saskia makes
flesh become red earth. —Or Hendrickje, crossing a stream, finds
shadow filling her white shift. Times when the body aches to be

found. The mobile clouds, filmic, shadowy over the patch-leaved
land. *Here*, to build a world sparking each moment as it trails to *was*.

Library of Water

On the highway, saw the eyes of a sheep staring through slats
of a trailer transport. And once visiting

someone in jail, saw all the hands reaching out from their cells
when a woman walked by. —Empty hands

grasping at air. One man kept saying, *Please, please,* a word
whose value seemed to decrease with others'

laughter, just as the Yamuna River laughs off steep rocks from its
Yamunotri Glacier source in the Himalayas

but turns to filth in the lower third of its 800-mile course
as it moves toward Delhi,

the stench of feces and chemical pollution creating a white froth. *We
are only passing through*

this earth. In Stykkisholmur, Iceland, there's a Library
of Water, a series of glass tubes, floor

to ceiling in length, each holding clear, melted water from one
of Iceland's glaciers. Imagine

if you were a child reading all their varieties of light, and when
the glaciers are gone how still

we will become in their aura as in a zoo with no animals.

3D

That our faces not become targets in the fray of living—
When the police kept kicking the black man, three of us
in unison screamed, *Stop.* They turned, then half-continued
as if their hate-batteries needed to be recharged, and I felt that I was
both inside and outside the event, watching, wearing 3D glasses
that created a depth of time, space, pain. A small amount of blood
kept mapping a faraway continent on his white shirt,
whose breast briefly became beast, a land where the *has been* and *would be*
seemed forever stalled, as in that village after the battle at Somme,
when the war was over, and on the street those two scraggly brothers
met—each thinking the other was dead—embraced, and together grew
tall, and on that hot June day shaded the entire town.

.

Family

I am dipping this spoon in honey, is what she said. Each of you
take it into your mouth and then pass it to the next person
until one of you will say, *I can no longer taste it,*
though perhaps you will, imagining you do, just as you imagine
that you can love again among the gathered years.

She was a great cook and before she died, even if she dipped
her finger into a cup of water it turned to broth. I was the last one
among siblings to take the spoon. *Yes,* I said. *I can taste it,*
although I couldn't. It starts

with a girl or boy—a strip of grass, a strip of sky—and the grass
either ends in a city, or someone keeps on walking, exploring what
wilderness is left, saying, *I remember.* —The woman

with walker, just outside Sonora, watering every morning
a patch of dead grass, watering and watering, her steady mindedness
a kind of freeing from that Dixie past.

—In Civita Castelana, the turtles alongside the fountain,
each one crawling onto the back of another, making
a small tower—losing, gaining foothold—as if they could

escape where? Hiking in the mountains, there was always one
snow-clad tarn he could not reach, or that high valley, sopping
green in sunlight, just a bit too far, but perfect like a grave in spring.

Why—

on the way to see her

for the first time at assisted living

do I get nervous, checking my hair,

my teeth for food? Why

do I keep humming a tune forgotten

for years? Why at the nurse's

station do I keep rearranging the blue irises, and why

when I say, Thank you for the *vase,*

does that word refuse to end, a whisper

in the silence suddenly overwhelmed by a TV's

drone. How do I approach her door now, only partway open—as if to contain

a new stillness? Now, seeing her asleep

in her wheelchair, I think how easy

it is in life to confuse happiness with freedom, but not

at the end. And how is it that from one cell dividing

I've returned again and again, and before promising now

to look for one sock in the lost and found, I lean forward and kiss her crooked

lipsticked mouth, and take both crepe-paper hands in mine

as though just getting ready to dance.

We

As if all our lives we are writing one sentence
whose letters begin large and become smaller and smaller.
My sentence begins in the mountains after a snowstorm
where I am using my entire body to form each letter
through the drifting snow. Others are watching
from the valley. We are all on our hands and knees,
squinting at the preposition "toward" near the sentence's
end. We are touching the windward vowels and broken remains
of consonants. We are on our hands and knees, crawling
through the sopping mud and snow-pocked earth. We
are trying to make out the last word, feasting like animals on its tall grass.

Faces

—touching their curves, ridges, hollows, holes
for ears, nose, mouth—the plump
cheeks and creased brow. To hold each face

close like a bowl or vase beneath clouds, and to keep
them from passing as I crouch by the gate, listening to the *knock,*
knocking on a door. *Yes,* I squeezed

paint right out of the tube onto the canvas. Yes, I put my face
into the garden's dirt when mother died. Yes, I pushed
another down and pulled her up

from sleep, our bodies floating through blue
flame while the past narrowed. There are so many stories
with faces in airports, plazas, or school

where those kids spilled honey, their heads
scrunched, licking it right off the counter with their
sticky laughs, their mouths growing

toward screams, marigolds on a grave, those faces
mapping what they've seen, tasted,
touched—scent of irises

bee-gilded, the mind drunk with the violent
hope of spring, and all the faces facing
rivers, hearing within green

all the lost, musty voices gathered in one tongue.

Hungry

Green for a long time then purple before everything turned black, spectral.
—The spandrel within the word *goodbye*, and the yellow
frisbee climbing beyond the yard and the boy

reaching. His entire body. —The truck. The mother screaming, *No*,
no, and the way she scratched her

fingernails into the dirt, deeper, as if she could catch hold and climb somewhere
out of it, or pull the earth's motion backward
till this didn't occur in the blaring

silence and red near-dusk where the driver
stood above the body—brief

monument, and we saw in that mother's
pouring grief the way memory
resists entropy

as she said, *Aaron, Aaron*—the sirens already tearing the name apart, she
remaining on all fours, resisting any hand, preferring

to be animal, staring at the grass, its thousand green lashes.
—Hungry, that night I dreamed
a bear had broken into the house and was ransacking

the fridge, but it was a cartoon bear and after a neighbor
ran over and shot twice, it slumped

on its haunches, leaning against the white enamel, bleeding,
laughing, groaning through the slow days
without dying. —Sniffing, our cats

approached, and it touched them with its giant pads, claws,
collecting sensory data from this world. There was

something so good as we approached with nothing but our hands.

Radiance

On the hill a man inside the ribs of a half-built house, that man
waving to me inside my half-built house, both of us on ladders, once
long ago. *Good morning*, he shouts that spring, as if from a dream,
only the *ping, ping, ping* of nails struck. Why do I remember it? The future
waxing for each of us putting in doors, windows, and skylights. Scent
of wet lumber drying in sunlight, as if ready to bloom as we open
something too big to see, and then the slow wind—furniture, kids, cats,
dogs, graduations, reunions—this puzzle each of us makes but can't quite
see the missing pieces spawned, or what later will be willed away. And what
of that radiance pouring through windows, blotching the walls at dusk
as I lift a daughter onto my lap, a daughter who will lift her daughter
while steadying my chair. Where's the hammer I dropped to find in the parish
of grass a bird's skull? —Its small balloon blown from bone wherein I glimpse snow,
spring greening, and others who will come, touching names carved in stone pooling
   light.

Wilderness

To come from a place in the Yukon where few maps exist and arrive in a city is no different than the birth of any infant, and the same country that sends a rocket to space sends youth to war. —Inner dark to outer dark, just like that, and within the joyful shine of things a rusty-white bike among noon-red hollyhocks. Rain, and then the bees slip back into their gloved rooms. —Sun, then rain on Jimmy's just-waxed Vette, the red one now in his parents' garage when the IED's blinking was lost in the flash and a joke torn from his lips. Back home they fold, refold, then present the flag beneath trees that now stand taller than people. *People*, so many of us trapped in that word. So many toppling over in grief, or life. One thinks of Marsden Hartley's painting *Christ Held by Half-Naked Men*, eight of them, all shirtless and buff in blue pants, form a triangle with one in front, seated, holding a chalky-green, womanized Christ. They're all stone-faced wearing hats and hands almost bear-pawed, while Christ, half-buff, spent, clings to his dangling crown as he's draped in the leader's lap. What's so tragic, because it's funny, is that they're sacrificing their bodies, stubborn in those hats. Big and stubborn as if to playfully birth him again. The painting hits you right in the solar plexus—gut nerves to brain. —A pietà of sorts, but more a force to bring him back to life—just for a moment—the way those soldiers do, helmeted, around their shrapnel-flayed-un-helmeted friend. *Jesus, what a mess,* you could say about both, and perhaps reason enough, if you did come from the Yukon, to return there and sit under the black spruce or naked aspens flanking a flagless high meadow in August.

Bright in June Sun

The young man, kneeling at his mother's tomb, lays red tulips there,

the young man wearing a too-big white shirt, one out of date, like those

on any thrift store rack, the shirt bright in June sun, so that from

a distance you see its cumulous cloud above the granite slab's

floating glare that could be a lake, where the boy, on a raft,

looks at a houseboat on fire, or that boy could be an astronaut

in his space suit adrift, still circling the ship, or look—he's a gull

pecking red flesh, or a polar bear, alone on an ice flow, but really

it's just a boy below that summer cloud where a toy jet ferries people away,

a boy bending above his mother's tomb, and it appears that space

is kneeling over time, but only because the latter has stopped.

III. WILD

Nike of Samothrace

—Her fish scales, her chains, the woman's headless
wings and blown

tunic of Parian marble. —The wet-see-thru
camisole. By sea she's

arrived, lighting on the ship's prow. One leg
thrust forward, the draped sails

of robes. (Somewhere near, between defeat and prayer, a drive-by
shooting. —The candy thrown around the body, the ambulance. They stole

the dead girl's dog, while far away outside Jakarta
in sweatshops some work for 20 cents an hour, and there's

one with his mouth taped shut in sunlight.) From a sanctuary
she was unearthed and taken to the Louvre

where on the grand Daru staircase she stands, stolen, moving
in several directions at once.

Legend

There are the old questions about animals on cave walls
and how words from blood and ochre
formed there, and the new questions about vanishing
species and how we will ever
speak them, how will we say, zebra,
when there are none? *When it becomes now,* we say about the future
collapsing. *Then,* in the past, sometimes we'd chew
on the grass, and the green
would cut our mouths—grass of the dead. Daylight keeps
surging from that one antler
on the French cave wall, and there's a breeze
in the midnight grass, while above, that comet's silver starburst mane
untangles time in space, fire to carbon, not unlike the waste
we make on earth, though the former writes a script
of light, the latter a book of darkness, and now we must eat
the book, even the glittering trash inside until we feel shadow
tide our blood, the buildings climb our faces and everything we see looks small.

All the tiny arrows

How the future's already veering toward yesterday. We are such
acrobats of the moment. When the dam's floodgates
broke, the fishermen thought about going back for their cars, but running
uphill, watched them float downstream. —Or the guest, after being invited
to dinner, insists that the host come to his house instead, the host
hit by a car in route—head injury—and three years later dies of a stroke. It's
not so much the one arrow of time, but all the tiny arrows shot at once
that confuse. Unlike the tadpole morphing into frog, there's a choice
at each moment. In the sky's black expanse, a puff of wind
seems to come after each brief comet, and the mind
is cleared of its weather—a dead friend—and I think how some poems
are like a good suicide. You can't know too much
before you start, but follow each rueful second blossoming
toward deeper shades of gray like a photo
underexposed in the darkroom, and I'm developing it now, the one
of the dead friend, and then I will frame it, place it in shadow
on a dark wall where sometimes a lightbulb will lob its dusks around
till they resemble snow clouds or a leaping animal, and now someone screams,
for it's from that wind that all words come, as we all keep moving
—unsure—through the jumbling debris of moments until each
of us becomes the one who enters memory, the one who has no age.

Just once

The pine's height and radius of shadow like a clock
over the land, then clouds, their brief but long age—centuries
dissolving, maps, people dispossessed of houses, things. The road
with me on it, runneled with time as the vivid present's
unleashed, even in a book—the invisible wind lifting slightly
the pronoun *I* while the white page buoys the iridescence
of being. —A starling bathing in a puddle, the indigo, ink-blue feathers
steeped in black. Water, yes, between the present and slow motion
past. Lakeside, Lynn still blowing out candles on a cake whose burnt
sugar we lick from spoons where our faces become wobbly. Wind
again, breaths around a table then *poof*, some are gone like this
small intaglio fish—the ancient light within a fossil—its
fading boundaries—Yours, mine. Now tiny wildfires across
the page as the yellow pines and blue spruce crown and people run,
drive through the smoke, ash of ruin. Fire, you can see right
through it like time. —Gold train of that baptismal gown, long, a section
added for each child passed through the pews toward the female pastor.
Members watching who'd worn the gown, and the Russian woman
who'd made it 60 years ago. A *go*, that's what we call this life, a marvelous
ride, no matter. —The same Aprils for all through sunlit rain, greening
even memory. *Just once* this moment like the verb "is" whose
slight hiss pollinates speech. When the downpour hit, we ran to a cave
where on our knees we mewled, touched—nothing but hands and mouths—
then walked out, strange beasts in sunlight, the *has been* and *would be* forever stalled.

Gift

Bending over the small wrapped box, the once-newlyweds find inside
    a tiny wrecking ball moving back & forth. They close

the box and remember when they were *new* and the time
    seemed raw, vulnerable like the yolk of a half-cooked egg,

and at night she would look up at the unheralded, cryptic
    stars that never explain, only *seem*. Yes, that they appear

greater through distance, just as the memory of a person
    can seem greater than his or her life. And yes, sometimes

he would like to open the box and stop the ball with his thumb, to tear
    it from its mount and cast it into a field of giant sunflowers

where the ball would need to be buried deep with a shovel just so they
    could see each twirling-slow-yellow mouth catch sunlight, a beauty

of such wreckage that no swinging forth & back between Yes & No could stop.

Livestream

From the tiny axles and balance wheels of an Elgin watch, to the Saturn
3-stage rocket, so many lives, and the way light continues to blow through memory.
Mid-May, the mulberries purpling, slowly falling in the drive, while the river
speaks and polishes names like stones. You can build a small city with them
or they can become lost among others—or you could skip one along an eddy
maybe 5, 7 times? *What luck* just to be here among rough-hewn, half-collapsed
settler-cabins where you can still hear the word "gold" hollow out the loneliness
in town names like St. Elmo—or Alta—at dusk as the high summer creek
rushes and Cassiopeia's wide *W* finds its glint then lofts in a dark wind,
I mean this flow, the known and unknown of all things falling—mayflies,
border walls, pamphlets, bombs, snow, currency, ash, or a chimpanzee's
"look" toward its keeper, while others quietly file through a lobby's
livestream feed, a new form of time that just delays the passing
the way bricks still hold in a ruined chimney. —This one of an old foundry,
everything vanished but that—brick against brick, hour against year—this
ghost town's grave, bell-less, voiceless, except for the waterfall, its
curtain half drawn. —Drawn with light, tongued. This town resembles a set
being dissembled. Sheds, houses unshelved, actorless except for the bear,
deer. —The hunger what keeps. The hunger like memory stubborn to go away.

English

The argument that English, its
speed, the language of business
is stripping specific identity
from other cultures, for example
when a Creole friend, lost in
Montreal, asks (in French) a stranger
for directions, he's told, *Speak
White*—both suddenly miffed.
Or try to imagine when the ziggurat
is just called a tower, I thought on
April 16, watching Notre-Dame in
flames, as tourists yelled, "The church
is on fire," as if the word *cathedral* had
burned, and *church* was that word's soot,
as if those bees fertilizing language,
flying from city to city, got lazy, settling
down in the suburbs. Must feel good
when the Inuit says, "anui," meaning snow used to
make water, not "apati," snow layered. Must
feel good to feel language fitting a need. Must
feel good, that precise taste of clean water.

Plaster of Paris

The chocolate melting in the sun. I untie the bow, take the clear wrapper off, smudging the dark on my fingers. I remember asking her the name of the elephant, before she died. She was the last one who would know. Years later, clearing out the house, I found the plaster cast of her hand that I'd made in art class. I dusted it off and thirty years later began to paint it as it was—the pink flesh tones, a pencil to make the knuckle-lines more fine, then some white on the crescent fingernails. In Paris later, I discovered that the plaster powder is named from the calcium sulfite mined near Montmartre. The elephant's name was Charley. Six years old, asked to feed it, I stuffed the entire plastic bag in his trunk. When I returned to the zoo with my father, 14 years later, the elephant remembered, dousing me with water. I keep the plaster hand in a sweater drawer. The resemblance too striking to keep out. It reaches slightly upward while slightly closed, as if it's caught something. The body's clock of blood and bone. I'm eating the chocolate now. My hand dark and sweet with it as I keep folding and unfolding the map of Paris.

Spring, 2020

Clouds cannot make enough sacred texts, and so much
depends on perspective. Do you want to keep the world behind you
or in front, ever forming? —Where you might also glimpse light
from the buckler's shield? —Whenever we celebrate a birthday now
I can't help thinking of the dead that made us. Are they in front,
opening? I love Robert Mapplethorpe's photo, *Apollo* (1988), taken
one year before his death   the white marble close-up of mouth,
nose, eyes gleaming in the ravenous light. How much was there
for him to hear or touch then? We live our lives between the towns
of Yes & No, but the towns become cities filled with *ifs* and *maybes*
waiting. April is all *yes*, green, streaming snow and rain-light. April—
yes, the thrill of its swift clouds, mud-lust, frowsy pink buds and memory.

Nearer

To keep arriving always, and the book we all want
will be written entirely in the present tense by someone
walking into the remaining green,

looking as into spring rain where sometimes
the dead appear as loose vowels or open
windows—*yes*—they

are summoning you just a little north of the present
where the puff of seconds sets stuff
in motion, as with

the aspirates and sibilants of certain words, and everything's
so close, it's invisible yet
thriving to be

seen, heard, smelled, felt, and licked into the whirling
May of revenants—tadpole, minnow, lacewings—
you can see

right thru. —Nearer us to them—as sun flames on ponds,
lakes. Nearer fire, blood,
phlegm. Nearer

                  waking, nearer,
          sleep, and how sheer
      their give or take.

Variation on a Phrase by Dickinson

Because I could not   stop, I remember how   I might have, Yes,

because I was always   hurrying to the next   thing, because I was

like you or   her, hurrying, I did   not—but maybe

paused over   the passing   white *while- space*

between parts   occurring, the way   a cloud, sky-

ward will, blurring   things together, or a-   part. I see clearly

now (not   really), but I am   sorry, so much

time did what time   does. A white shirt gone—   brief through glare.

Trailer for a Movie not yet Made

People are being herded from suburban neighborhoods into stadiums
and convention centers. They are given

    * * *

cots, soup, bread, and told stories of how to ritualize
space. They colonize

    * * *

like ants and task quickly while being surveilled. Just as
one woman says she has touched

    * * *

the mother lava, there's a great flash and everyone outside
—along with the trees, and cars arriving—is

    * * *

stilled as if by lightning, and photographed
at that instant when the movie

    * * *

cuts to just before the final scene, 100 years later,
where the constellations shine

    * * *

in different positions and everyone's moving in slow
motion like fish through water, recording

    * * *

light, touching faces, then turning in a vast
current of understanding, an intuition before bodies. It was

* * *

April, and I felt something like an invisible ticket
so big I could not hold its green in my hands.

1937 Indian Head Nickel

Flipped into the air & now catching
Sun in the palm

of one Hand, *there*, its aura—rainbow-hued, as above
that Mesa after rain.
Buffalo

shot from a train. The coin's small
tribunal, envoy. "You might as well expect rivers
to run backwards

as anyone born free to be
content. . ."[1] Each

buffalo's mass the weight
of place & hole in the air.

1. Chief Joseph, Nez Perce

La liberté libre

When I read Rimbaud's letter, written at the age of 16, the one to Izambard
saying how much he "loves *free freedom*";

Rimbaud who had just arrived home, the one he would leave a hundred times;

Rimbaud ready to sell his watch for a ticket anywhere, Rimbaud quivering
like a drawn arrow, his cheeks flushed, "The Drunken Boat" already
written with its roiled visions on the open sea;

when I read this letter, I remember the hives in spring and how some bees
would swarm, leaving their hexagonal mansions of wax, leaving
their brood and powdered bee bread in the dusk-yellow

glow, leaving everything for a new place, with nothing, the way the poet did,
un-singing his *Illuminations*, the sillage of their imagination

spreading across France, Europe, while unlike the queen who always swarms
to a darker place, hollow log or tree trunk, he traveled

to brighter ones—Sumatra, Cyprus, Addis Ababa, Aden, Harar, Choa—trading
coffee, spices, hides, and camels, often walking 20 miles a day, a feral path,

unhooking places from their maps the way he once unhooked words
from the Latin, Greek, French;

Rimbaud *the other*, othering far, the force of his body through the fierce light.

Thirst

To bear the years, ever the minutes. Last time I saw

you, running the tap water cold into a glass we

both drank from the sky too heaving clouds, wind

following your hair while above a plane cast its transom

of shadow. Who are you now? I ask, reading the Obit, & how

the glass held for a while our fingerprints. *Reach, reach*

is how my mind finds you. Door by door this life, then afterglow.

Pinprick

You are growing more and more deeply into your name, time
creating cavernous spaces between vowel and consonant.
—To go on seeing in the dark. Not to see objects, but the hall
of time that grows both longer and shorter, where perhaps one
or two stray ghosts come for shelter, and linger, drinking
a deeper dark from your dark, a bridge just beyond memory,
and they are building something there, the smallest house where
bone-hungry for earth they are waving their filmy arms, inviting
you to the infinitely small glow they've made, a pinprick
of fire *yessing* this, *yessing* that, and you would love to get down
on your knees, open the door with your finger, and while watching,
tell them how all the land's vast green devours the light in tiny sips.

Three Panels

1.

They are sitting at a table with two flat river stones between them. Each moves one stone, in turns, toward the other. His long hair covers part of the table and begins to gray as she considers a move. The color of the room changes from light to dark many times, and then there is one person and two stones.

2.

It's the "o" in the word God that slightly holds, deep inside the most inner part where one can't see any border, where crawling again, saying, *hello, hello,* and touching, waiting to enter one another's body, they feel that tightly-wound letter's wind.

3.

And the first space was of earth, coursing water, and from mud—a bourgeoning of green, corolla to petal lifting pollen, bee; and the second space was of flesh, a newt climbing a wet rock ashore—then trees, doors, beds, the woods of pleasure, pain, their bodies; and the third space was not of *is,* but of what could be, of *if,* and every cloud shifting, doing in its undoing.

Yet

Climbing the glacier's bulk of time and glare, where wind makes
light—till a cloud passes years and some of us are gone. —This brief
blindness until descending, she sees the lichen's wild
green blooming on a rock, the crack in a dropped yellow
pencil, and the ruddy snowflower stubborn by a pine as the rain insists
through sunlight, an ephemeral door for everything

not body. There is the town below painted small
with its boxes for eating, sleeping, and souvenirs, with its white-steepled
box for prayer, and as she drinks between rocks the cold, slate-tasting water,
someone is already dismantling some of those boxes
in order to make bigger ones called *city*, and so she turns, hiking the sun
up and the sun down, hiking until the only thing she knows

is humus and root-scent, until she's so far within the joinery
of limbs as to be beyond all story, until the half-dead branches of cedars
look like ancient archers, and when carving a stake tent
she cuts herself, that blood on stone where the grass sweeps
seems like a new world, and this too is a kind of new story—where in dusk
the voiceless vireo would call—but not yet.

Refrain

Let me be silent, looking at these newborns, each one's
　　small *thump de Thump* and blush, electric & rose
at once; let me be silent as during that snowstorm

　　between Cerro summit and Cimarron when I pulled off
Rt. 50 onto a forest road where seven elk gathered around—
　　huffing, grunting, mewling—taking warmth from the car,
gently knocking their antlers, their dark brown collars and beards

　　dripping. —Silent, as when the one, who once carried me on his shoulders,
lay in his coffin, dressed in a light blue jacket like a rocket
　　blasting off into the sky's throat. —Silent, as the word *August*

is swallowed in its own slow hush. Let me be silent,
　　entering that chancel of sunlit pines where the chanterelles invisibly
step, spreading their spores. Let me be silent as when once on a hill I glimpsed
　　my own house from a distance and was surprised, and kept on walking.

Notes

"The smaller house" is for Derek Sheffield.

"Nike of Samothrace," representing the goddess Victory, prominently on display on the Daru staircase of the Louvre Museum, was excavated in 1863 on the Greek island of Samothrace by the French vice-consul and amateur archaeologist Charles Champoiseau.

"Livestream" is for Tom Sleigh.

"English" is partially based on a brief encounter narrated by Alain Borer in his book *De quel amour blessée: Réflexions sur la langue française* (Gallimard, 2014).

"Spring, 2020." "Buckler's shield" references the language in Psalm 91.

"Variation on a Phrase by Dickinson" loosely references Dickinson's "Because I could not stop for Death" (#712) c. 1863.

"1937 Indian Head Nickel." The statement is attributed to Chief Joseph, Nez Perce.

"La liberté libre" is for Alain Borer

Acknowledgments

Many thanks to the editors who first published these poems:

"Nike of Samothrace" appeared in *Academy of American Poets*.

"Vertigo" appeared in *Agni Review*.

"*Alive*" and "All the tiny arrows" appeared in *American Poetry Review*.

"Balloon," "Edges," and "Gift" appeared in *Conjunctions* (40th Anniversary Issue).

"Library of Water," "Story," and "The Life" appeared in *Conjunctions* (online).

"Wilderness" appeared in *The Experiment Will Not Be Bound: An Anthology of Contemporary American Poetry*

"Family" and "*Just Once*" appeared in *Great River Review*.

"Hungry," "Legend," "Nearer," and "La liberté libre" appeared in *Interim*.

"Thirst" and "Three Panels" appeared in *New American Writing*.

"Goes" and "1937 Indian Head Nickel" appeared in *The Los Angeles Review*.

"Plaster of Paris" appeared in *Pleiades*.

"Bright in June Sun" appeared in *Plume* (online).

"Ash" appeared in *Plume 9 Anthology*.

"How Long?" and "Tree, River" appeared in *Poetry Northwest*.

"Light" and "Notre-Dame of Paris, 2019" appeared in *Pratik*.

"The Dead" appeared in *The Southern Review*.

"The smaller house" appeared in *The Sun*.

Special thanks to Angie Estes, David Keplinger, and Jennifer Sweeney, who read and commented on these poems in manuscript form, and to my colleagues in the Levan Institute for the Humanities Environmental Humanities working group.

About the Author

MARK IRWIN is an award-winning author who has published eleven poetry collections. He is a professor of English at the University of Southern California where he teaches in the PhD in Creative Writing & Literature Program. Irwin has received numerous awards for his writing, including The Nation/Discovery Award, four Pushcart Prizes, two Colorado Book Awards, the James Wright Poetry Award, the Philip Levine Prize for Poetry, and fellowships from the National Endowment for the Arts and the Fulbright, Lilly, and Wurlitzer Foundations. His published works include *Shimmer, A Passion According to Green, American Urn: Selected Poems,* and *Bright Hunger.* His poetry has appeared in many literary magazines including *The American Poetry Review, Agni Review, The Atlantic Monthly, Conjunctions, The Kenyon Review, Paris Review, Poetry, The Nation, New American Writing, The New Republic, The New York Times,* and *The Southern Review.*